ENGLISH ON CALL

LEVEL TWO

Victoria F. Kimbrough

Marjorie Vai

McGRAW–HILL, INC.

New York St. Louis San Francisco Auckland Bogotá
Caracas Hamburg Lisbon London Madrid Mexico
Milan Montreal New Delhi Paris San Juan
São Paulo Singapore Sydney Tokyo Toronto

English On Call: Level Two

1 2 3 4 5 6 7 8 9 0 MAL MAL 9 6 5 4 3 2

ISBN 0-07-066784-5

This book was typeset by Phyllis Wright.
The editors were Roseanne Mendoza, Leslie Berriman, Mary Gill, Celine-Marie Pascale, Karen Davy, and Leslie Nolan.
The production supervisor was Diane Baccianini.
The photo researcher was Judy Mason.
The illustrators were Barbara Lehman, James Hoston, Rick Hackney, Bill Border, and Anica Gibson.
The cover was illustrated by Barbara Lehman.
The design and art directors were Leslie Nolan and Francis Owens.

Library of Congress Cataloging-in-Publication Data

Kimbrough, Victoria, 1943–
    English on call: level two / Victoria F. Kimbrough, Marjorie Vai.
        p.   cm.
    1. English language—Textbooks for foreign speakers.   2. English
language—Grammar—1950–   I. Vai, Marjorie. II. Title.
PE1128.K46 1991
428.2'4—dc20   91-23727
                                                                          CIP

Grateful acknowledgment is made for use of the following:

Photographs *Page 6* © George W. Gardner/Stock, Boston; *7* © Davidson/The Image Works; *12 (left)* © Cary Wolinsky/Stock, Boston; *(right)* © L. Fleming/The Image Works; *16 (left* and *right)* © IRA Kirschenbaum/Stock, Boston; *84* © UPI/Bettmann; *112* © The Bettmann Archive.

Contents

Introduction   *v*

Unit 1   *1*
Count and Noncount Nouns

Unit 2   *9*
The Comparative—Adjectives

Unit 3   *16*
The Superlative—Adjectives

Unit 4   *23*
Will

Unit 5   *30*
Should and *Would*

Unit 6   *38*
Past Progressive

Unit 7   *44*
Adverbial Time Clauses

Unit 8   *54*
Must and *Might*

Unit 9   *62*
Verbs Followed by Gerunds or Infinitives

Unit 10   *68*
Present Perfect

Unit 11   *78*
Simple Past vs. Present Perfect

Unit 12   *84*
Present Perfect Progressive

Unit 13   *90*
Could and *Would*

Unit 14   *98*
Direct and Indirect Objects

Unit 15   *106*
Past Perfect

Introduction

English On Call is a three-level computer software/workbook series designed for student, young adult, and adult learners of English. Each of the fifteen units in the three levels consists of contextualized exercises that use humor, drama, general-interest topics, and even mystery to present and practice individual grammar points. In order to enhance students' awareness of natural spoken English, all the activities in the software and many exercises in the workbooks are presented in a continuous dialogue format written in a casual conversational style. Learner control, active language manipulation, and the development of learning strategies have been emphasized in the design of *English On Call* software.

Unit Organization and Content

Each unit is divided into three parts, as follows:

- *Workbook activities include recognition exercises that introduce the meaning and form of a structure, a grammar box that summarizes this information, and exercises that give students practice using the structure in meaningful contexts.*

- *Software activities include interactive presentations of the structure, contextualized grammar exercises, and text-reconstruction activities.*

- *More challenging follow-up workbook exercises give students the opportunity to see how the structure works in additional contexts. This section often includes open-ended, personalized activities.*

Although the software and workbook at each level are designed to be used together, both may also be used independently. A workbook unit provides sufficient coverage of each grammar point to stand on its own; and since the software units contain both a presentation and a grammar box along with the exercises, they can easily be plugged into any program as an independent supplement.

Classroom Uses

The software/workbook units may function in one or more of the following ways:

- *As individualized instruction for students who may be having problems with specific structures or concepts.*

- *As additional practice and reinforcement of structures in a contextualized and conversational format for full-class participation.*

- *As review and catch-up work for students who have already been exposed to the material at a different time and perhaps in a different learning environment.*

Series Organization and Content

An attempt has been made to control the use of vocabulary and secondary structures within the units so that they need not necessarily be presented in the sequence in which they appear in each level. Teachers and students should be able to pick and choose according to the needs of their curriculum. The structures included at each level are as follows:

Level One (beginning to low-intermediate)

Tenses and Modals
Simple Present–*to be*
Simple Present–all verbs
Simple Past
Present Progressive
Simple Present vs. Present Progressive
Can
Future with *going to*

Other Points
There is, There are
Subject Pronouns
WH- questions
Possessive Adjectives and Possessive Pronouns
Possessive Forms of Nouns
Adverbs of Frequency
Object Pronouns

Level Two (intermediate)

Tenses and Modals
Will
Should and *Would*
Past Progressive
Might and *Must*
Present Perfect
Simple Past vs. Present Perfect
Present Perfect Progressive
Would and *Could*
Past Perfect

Other Points
Direct and Indirect Objects
Comparatives and Superlatives
Adverbial Clauses
Gerund vs. Infinitive

Level Three (high-intermediate to advanced)

Tenses and Modals
Reported Speech
Passive Voice
Past Modals
Real Conditional
Unreal Conditional–Present and Past
Causative Verbs–Active and Passive
Future Perfect

Other Points
Noun Clauses
Relative Clauses

1 *Read the sentences. Then look at the information from Rick Daly's geography book and write the correct sentences under each map.*

- There aren't many people per square mile.
- There are a lot of trees.
- They don't have much rain.
- There are a lot of rivers.
- There isn't much oil.
- They don't have many trees.

- They have a lot of oil.
- They produce a lot of coffee.
- They don't have many rivers.
- They have a lot of iron.
- They have a lot of rain.
- There isn't much land that can be used for agriculture.

BRAZIL

Forest

SAUDI ARABIA

Forest

BRAZIL
Population: 143,277,000 (43 people per sq. mi.)
Size: 3,287,487 sq. mi. Major products: coffee, sugar cane, cocoa, oranges, bananas. Has the largest iron ore deposit in the world, but imports most of its oil. Annual rainfall: Amazon region 80–140 in. Northeast region 10–65 in. Central & southern regions 50 in.

SAUDI ARABIA
Population: 11,519,000 (13 people per sq. mi.)
Size: 839,996 sq. mi. Major product: oil (produces 1/4 of the world's oil supply); only 1% of the land is used for agriculture, so imports most of its food.
Annual rainfall: 3–4 in.

1. a. *They produce a lot of coffee.*

   b. _____

   c. _____

   d. _____

   e. _____

   f. _____

2. a. _____

   b. _____

   c. _____

   d. _____

   e. _____

   f. _____

2 *There are some nouns that you can count. For example, you can say "I have a book" or "I have two books." These nouns have a singular form (book) and a plural form (books). There are other nouns that you can't count, so they have no plural form; words like sugar, salt, corn, gold, and snow are noncount nouns. The following words are from Exercise 1. Write them in the correct column.*

iron	rain	coffee	river
oil	person (people)	land	tree

Count nouns

_____

_____

_____

_____

Noncount nouns

_____

_____

_____

_____

3 *Look again at the information in Exercise 1. Then answer these questions.*

1. How many people live in Brazil? _____

2. How many people live in Saudi Arabia? _____

3. How much land is used for agriculture in Saudi Arabia? _____

4. How much oil does Saudi Arabia produce? _____

5. About how much rain does Saudi Arabia get every year? _____

6. How many inches of rain fall in the Amazon region annually? _____

7. About how much rain does the northeast region of Brazil get

   every year? _____

BRAZIL
Population: 143,277,000 (43 people per sq. mi.)
Size: 3,287,487 sq. mi. Major products: coffee, sugar cane, cocoa, oranges, bananas. Has the largest iron ore deposit in the world, but imports most of its oil. Annual rainfall: Amazon region 80–140 in. Northeast region 10–65 in. Central & southern regions 50 in.

SAUDI ARABIA
Population: 11,519,000 (13 people per sq. mi.)
Size: 839,996 sq. mi. Major product: oil (produces 1/4 of the world's oil supply); only 1% of the land is used for agriculture, so imports most of its food. Annual rainfall: 3–4 in.

4 *After geography class, Rick went to Hamburger Heaven for lunch. Read the conversation. Then put the underlined words in the correct column. If a noun is plural or preceded by* **a/an** *or* **one**, *it is a count noun.*

WAITRESS: Can I help you?

RICK: I'd like a <u>hamburger</u>, please.

WAITRESS: Do you want <u>cheese</u> on it?

RICK: Yes, please. And I'd like some <u>french fries</u>, too. Oh, and some iced <u>tea</u>.

WAITRESS: I'm sorry, but we don't have any iced tea.

RICK: Well, then, can I have some <u>coffee</u>, please?

WAITRESS: A <u>cup</u> or a <u>pot</u>?

RICK: Just a cup. With some <u>milk</u> and <u>sugar</u>.

WAITRESS: OK. Do you want <u>onions</u> and <u>pickles</u> on your burger?

RICK: I don't want pickles, but onions are OK. And some <u>mayonnaise</u>, please. And can I have some <u>ketchup</u> for my fries? And for dessert, do you have any chocolate <u>ice cream</u>?

WAITRESS: Sorry. We don't have any ice cream, but I can give you a <u>piece</u> of chocolate cake. It's delicious.

RICK: That sounds great.

Count nouns

hamburger

Noncount nouns

cheese

Count and Noncount Nouns

Count nouns have both a singular and a plural form:

Singular	Plural
a pencil	some pencils
one pencil	two pencils
	many pencils
	a lot of pencils

Noncount nouns have only one form:

paper
some paper
much paper
a lot of paper

With count nouns, use *some, a lot of, many.*
With noncount nouns, use *some, a lot of, much.*

Note: Use *any* with both count and noncount nouns in questions; use *some* in affirmative responses and *any* in negative responses. *Much* and *many* are usually used in questions and negative responses.

Do you have any { pencils / paper } ?   Yes, we have some. / No, we don't have any.

Do you drink much coffee?   I don't drink much during the week, but I drink a lot on the weekend.

5 *The cook at Hamburger Heaven makes delicious spaghetti. He usually cooks enough for 100 people at a time. Read his recipe and the list of supplies. Then complete the conversation. Use* **some, any, how much, how many** *or information from the recipe and list.*

SHOPPER: What do we need for tomorrow?

COOK: Well, we don't have _____ carrots, and we need
                1
_____ ground meat and _____ sugar.
      2   3

SHOPPER: Do we have _____ bay leaves?
                 4

COOK: No. We're out of bay leaves. And I think we're going to need
_____ onions and garlic.
      5

SHOPPER: Do we have _____ peppercorns left?
               6

COOK: Yes, there are a lot.

SHOPPER: OK. _____ carrots do we need?
       7

COOK: We need only _____ for tomorrow, but why don't you get
              8
2 dozen?

SHOPPER: And _____ ground meat do I get?
         9

COOK: We need _____. And get 25 pounds of sugar and a big jar
         10
of bay leaves.

SHOPPER: OK. And _____ garlic and tomato paste do you want?
         11

COOK: We need _____ of garlic and _____ of tomato paste.
₁₂ ₁₃

SHOPPER: _____ cans of tomatoes do we need?
₁₄

COOK: _____.
₁₅

Now you're ready for the computer. When you finish at the computer, go to the next exercise.

6 *Sarah and Tim Brodsky are planning a trip to Mexico. The travel agent gave them some brochures about two interesting towns. Read the information and complete the first brochure with **a**, **some**, or **any**.*

Tula, Mexico   Population: 6,000

Main attraction—the archeological site 1 mile outside of town. It contains 2 pyramids, a palace, and several other buildings. The most famous pyramid is the Pyramid of Quetzalcóatl with its columns carved to look like Indian warriors. The town has several small, inexpensive hotels and some small, simple restaurants. The average hotel costs from $25 to $40 a night.

Tula is _____ small town north of Mexico City. There aren't _____ big
₁ ₂

hotels there, and there aren't _____ big, expensive restaurants. There aren't
₃

_____ beaches either. But people go there because there's _____
₄ ₅

wonderful archeological site near the town. At this site there are _____ beautiful
₆

pyramids and other structures that the Toltecs built about 1,000 years ago. Tula isn't

far from Mexico City, so most tourists don't spend the night there. But if you want to

stay, there are _____ very nice, small, clean hotels.
₇

Now complete this brochure with **much, many,** *or* **a lot (of).** *You will see that sometimes, in exercises like this one, there are two correct answers.*

Cancún, Mexico   Population: 60,000

There are over 30 big hotels on the beach—most with bars, discotheques, swimming pools, and beautiful beaches. The cost of a one-day stay in a hotel on the beach is from $80 to $160. Plane fare from New York is about $290 round trip.

Cancún is a small island off the east coast of Mexico. There are _____ big hotels
                                                                    8
and _____ wonderful beaches there. There's _____ nightlife too.
        9   10
There aren't _____ movie theaters and there aren't _____ concert
                  11   12
halls, but there are _____ bars and discotheques. Of course, life in Cancún is
                          13
expensive. It doesn't take _____ money to get there from New York, but it
                                    14
takes _____ money to stay there.
          15

7 *Complete these questions with* **much** *or* **many.** *Then answer the questions using the information in Exercise 6.*

1. How _____ pyramids are there in the ruins at Tula?

_____

2. How _____ money do you need to stay in a good, clean hotel in Tula?

_____

3. Are there _____ bars in Cancún? _____

   _____

4. Are there _____ movie theaters? _____

   _____

5. About how _____ money do you need to stay in a good hotel in Cancún?

   _____

8 *Write a paragraph about your own town or city. Use some of these words:* a/an, some, any, much, many, a lot (of). *You can look at the brochures on pages 6 and 7 if you need help.*

_____

_____

_____

_____

_____

_____

_____

_____

_____

_____

_____

_____

_____

_____

1 *Look at the pictures and complete the conversation with* **the bus** *or* **the plane.**

A: How are you getting to Miami?

B: I don't know yet. _____ is a lot faster than _____, but
   ₁   ₂

   it's more expensive too.

A: That's true. And at this time of year, _____ is more crowded than
                                              ₃

   _____. _____ will probably be more comfortable.
      ₄   ₅

B: I know. The people on _____ are usually less interesting than the
                               ₆

   people on _____ too. I always meet interesting people on
                  ₇

   _____.
      ₈

A: Well, how much time do you have? You know, _____ takes 36 hours.
                                                    ₉

B: Yes, I know. But then, _____ is cheaper and more interesting than
                               ₁₀

   _____, and _____ is less comfortable!
      ₁₁   ₁₂

2 *Look at the pictures and complete the sentences with the correct word.*

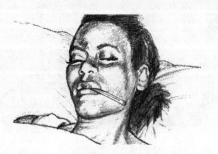

Yesterday

Today

1. My cold is _____ today
(better / worse)
than it was yesterday.

2. Yesterday I felt _____
(better / worse)
than I do today.

Last winter

This winter

3. Last winter wasn't as

_____ as this winter.
(cold / warm)

4. For people who like to ski, this

winter is _____
(better / worse)
than last winter.

The Comparative—Adjectives

The forms of the adjectives below are used to compare two things or persons.

For adjectives with:

1 syllable*	**2 or more syllables**
adjective + -er (+ than)	more + adjective (+ than)
bigger (than)	more beautiful (than)
finer (than)	more comfortable (than)

The blue dress is made of silk and costs $85.
The red dress is made of cotton and costs $150.

The blue dress is **finer** than the red dress, but the red dress is **more expensive.**

For comparing with:

good → better (than) bad → worse (than)

Tom got 95 on his exam. Jane got 90 on hers. Bill got 70 on his.
Tom's grade is **better** than Jane's, but Bill's is **worse.**

For comparing people or things **that** are:

Equal	**Not Equal**
as + adjective + as	not as + adjective + as
as long as	not as intelligent as

Tom and Paul are 5 feet 6 inches tall. Joe is only 5 feet tall.
Tom is **as** tall **as** Paul. Joe is **not as** tall **as** Tom and Paul.

*Spelling Rules: When an adjective ends in a single consonant preceded by a single vowel, the consonant is doubled: big → bigger.

When a 2 syllable adjective ends in y preceded by a consonant, change the y to i before adding -er: happy → happier.

When an adjective ends in e, add only an r:
fine → finer.

3 *Amy, Rick Daly's older sister, is talking to Tomiko, a student at City College.*
They are talking about the differences between New York and Kansas City. Complete
the conversation with the correct form of the adjective in parentheses.

TOMIKO: Of course New York is _more exciting_ than Kansas City, but Kansas
                        (1. exciting)

City is _____. And I think it's _____ than
        (2. relaxing)   (3. pretty)

New York too.

AMY: Yes, I always think of New York as _____ than Kansas City.
                                              (4. busy)

Life is _____ there. It's probably _____.
        (5. fast)   (6. interesting)

Certainly the people who live in New York are _____—let's
                                                  (7. strange)

say _____—than people in Kansas City, but Kansas City
     (8. original)

has its advantages too.

TOMIKO: It sure does. First of all, it's a lot _____ than New York and
                                                    (9. clean)

it isn't nearly as _____.
                    (10. dangerous)

AMY: It isn't as _____ as New York either. People pay over $1,000
                      (11. expensive)

for a one-bedroom apartment in New York!

TOMIKO: There is one big advantage to living in New York though. It's

_____ to get around there. The public transportation system
(12. easy)

in New York is much _____ than the one here. If you don't
                      (13. good)

have a car here, you can't move!

Now you're ready for the computer. When you finish at the computer, go to the next exercise.

4 *Look at the pictures and write sentences comparing the two young men. You may want to use* **probably** *or* **I think** *in some of your sentences. Use some of these adjectives:* **thin, heavy, organized, messy, good-looking, athletic, artistic, interesting, vain.** *For example:*

I think Jeff is more _____interesting_____ than Doug.

Doug probably isn't as _____artistic_____ as Jeff.

Jeff

Doug

1. _____

2. _____

3. _____

4. _____

5. _____

6. _____

7. _____

Now write sentences comparing two of your friends or family members. For example:

My father is more organized than my mother, but he isn't as creative as she is.

1. _____

2. _____

3. _____

4. _____

5. _____

5 *Look at the chart and write sentences about the four cars. Use adjectives like* **big/small, heavy/light, powerful, fast/slow, economical, cheap/expensive.** *Also use these words:* **more, less,** *and* **as.** *For example:*

The Mauriac isn't as economical as the Gazelle.
The Gazelle is less powerful than the Flash.
The Gazelle is cheaper than all the other cars.

Brand		Seats	Weight in lbs.	Cylinders	Top speed	Mi. per gal.	Price
Mauriac		7	3,254	8	130 m.p.h.	10	$14,999
Lightning		2	2,607	8	150 m.p.h	12	$11,459
Flash		5	2,900	6	100 m.p.h	32	$ 9,750
Gazelle		4	2,200	4	80 m.p.h	40	$ 6,989

1. _____

2. _____

3. _____

4. _____

5. _____

6. _____

7. _____

6 *Write sentences comparing cars that you know.*

1. _____

2. _____

3. _____

4. _____

5. _____

6. _____

1 *Circle the correct answer.*

Cheetah

Mount Everest

1. The largest ocean in the world is the

   a. Pacific. **b.** Atlantic. **c.** Arctic.

2. The smallest continent in the world is

   a. Europe. **b.** Africa. **c.** Australia.

3. The biggest country in the world is

   a. China. **b.** Canada. **c.** the Soviet Union.

4. The highest mountain in the world is

   a. Mt. Whitney. **b.** Mt. Kilimanjaro. **c.** Mt. Everest.

5. The longest river in the world is the

   a. Nile. **b.** Amazon. **c.** Mississippi.

6. The largest island in the world is

   a. Australia. **b.** Greenland. **c.** Japan.

7. The biggest city in the world is

   a. Tokyo. **b.** Sao Paulo. **c.** Mexico City.

8. The tallest building in the world is the

   a. Sears Tower in Chicago.
   b. World Trade Center in New York.
   c. Empire State Building in New York.

9. The fastest animal in the world is the

   a. tiger.
   b. cheetah.
   c. lion.

10. The hardest mineral is

   a. diamond.
   b. iron.
   c. quartz.

2 *What do you think? Answer these questions.*

1. Who's the most beautiful woman in the world? _____

2. Who's the best-looking man in the world? _____

3. Who's the best actor or actress in the world or in your country? _____

   _____

4. Who's the worst singer/actor/actress? _____

5. Who's the most intelligent person in your family? _____

   _____

6. Who's the most creative person in your family? _____

   _____

7. Which of your friends is the most unusual? _____

   _____

The Superlative—Adjectives

The forms of the adjectives below are used to compare three or more things or persons. Always use *the* with the superlative.

For adjectives with:

1 syllable*	**2 or more syllables**
adjective + *-est*	*most* + adjective
the biggest	the most beautiful
	the least beautiful

For comparing with:

good → *the best*   *bad* → *the worst*

Jane is 12 years old. Tim is 10 years old. Peter is 18 years old.
Peter is the oldest of the three. Tim is the youngest.

The Murphys' house costs $70,000. The Sotos' house costs $90,000. The Youngs' house costs $100,000.

The Youngs' house is the most expensive house on the block. The Murphys' house is the least expensive.

*Spelling Rules: When an adjective ends in a single consonant preceded by a single vowel, the consonant is doubled: big → biggest.

When a 2 syllable adjective ends in *y* preceded by a consonant, change the *y* to *i* before adding *-est:* happy → happiest.

When an adjective ends in *e*, add only an *st:* fine → finest.

3 Complete this newspaper article with the superlative forms of the adjectives in parentheses.

Traveling Salespeople Report

by Ann Daly

In a recent survey, traveling salespeople told what they thought of their customers in different parts of the U.S. They said that _____ place to (1. bad) do business was Boston because the people there were _____ . On the other hand, they (2. unfriendly) thought that _____ people lived in San (3. friendly) Francisco. They felt that the people in New York were _____ . "If you try to talk to a New (4. nervous) Yorker," one said, "he thinks you're trying to rob him or make him buy something he doesn't want!"

The people in Cleveland are _____ (5. apologetic) about their city. They are constantly telling you what's wrong with it. Most traveling salespeople thought that people in Chicago were _____ (6. difficult) to do business with, and that, in general, the people on the West Coast were _____ to (7. easy) deal with.

4 Stereotypes are ways of talking about people in general. Are there any stereotypes about people in your country? Here is a stereotype about some people in the United States:

People from Missouri are the most disbelieving people in the United States. (They don't believe anything.)

Write sentences like this one about people in your country. You might want to use some of these adjectives: **stingy, boring, hard-working, friendly, unfriendly, happy, polite, impolite, snobbish (stuck-up), disbelieving, religious.**

1. _____
2. _____
3. _____
4. _____

Now you're ready for the computer. When you finish at the computer, go to the next exercise.

5 *Write questions with the words in parentheses, using a superlative form in each question. Then look at the planet information and answer the questions.*

Planet	Size (in diameter)	Distance from sun (in millions of miles)	Estimated surface temperature	Time to orbit sun
Mercury	3,100 mi.	36.0	650° F.	88 days
Venus	7,700 mi.	67.2	675° F.**	224.7 days
Earth	7,927 mi.	92.9	59° F.	365 days
Mars	4,220 mi.	141.5	−80° F.**	687 days
Jupiter	88,700 mi.	483.4	−190° F.	12 years
Saturn	75,100 mi.	886.0	−235° F.	29.5 years
Uranus	32,000 mi.	1,782.0	−335° F.	84 years
Neptune	31,000 mi.	2,792.0	−360° F.	164.8 years
Pluto	4,000 mi.**	3,664.0	−370° F.**	247.7 years

* Near the equator at noon
** Some doubt about figures

1. _____
   (what / big / planet / in our solar system)
   _____

2. _____
   (what / small / planet / in our solar system)
   _____

3. _____
   (which planet / close / to the sun)
   _____

4. _____
   (which planet / far / from the sun)
   _____

5. _____
   (what / hot / planet / in our solar system)
   _____

6. _____
   (what / cold / planet / in our solar system)
   _____

7. _____
   (which planet / has / short / year)

6 *Complete the paragraph with the superlative forms of the adjectives in parentheses.*

One of _____ and _____ planets in our solar system is
       (1. interesting)   (2. unusual)

Saturn. It isn't _____ nor is it _____, but it is certainly
         (3. big)   (4. cold)

_____. This is because it's surrounded by rings, so it's difficult to
(5. mysterious)

see. In the past, astrologers thought that Saturn was the planet with _____
                                                  (6. negative)

influence and that people born under the sign of Saturn (Capricorns) were pessimistic.

7 *Amy's friend Janet is thinking about visiting Amy in Barker. Amy is telling her about the town. Complete the telephone conversation with the superlative forms of the adjectives in parentheses.*

AMY: Well, Barker is pretty small. _____ building in town is only
                                      (1. tall)

five stories high, and _____ building, the bank, is only about
                         (2. big)

8,000 square feet.

JANET: What's _____ thing to do?
           (3. interesting)

AMY: I guess it depends on what you like to do. _____ thing we can
                               (4. unusual)

do is to go see the old wagon-train trail. That's one of _____
                                          (5. famous)

attractions around here. You can still see the marks of the pioneer wagons! We have

a nice little museum too, four or five beautiful parks, and lots of good restaurants.

JANET: Where's _____ place to eat?
           (6. good)

AMY: Well, _____ place is Dave's Café. They have great hamburgers
         (7. cheap)

and apple pie. They have _____ breakfasts, though. A
                          (8. bad)

_____ restaurant is the Ranch House. It is also _____.
(9. good)   (10. expensive)

It has _____ steaks in Kansas.
       (11. good)

JANET: That sounds great. I'm hungry already. Is there anything exciting to do?

AMY: I guess _____ thing to do is to go into Kansas City. We can go
           (12. exciting)

to a concert or to a play. Or we can go dancing.

8 *Imagine that a friend is coming to visit you. Write him or her a paragraph telling about your town or city. Tell about the most interesting and exciting things to do, the best places to eat or to stay, the most unusual things to see or do, etc.*

_____

_____

_____

_____

_____

_____

_____

_____

1 *These people are having their fortunes told. Read the sentences. Then look at the pictures and write the correct sentences under each picture.*

- You'll live on a tropical island.
- You'll meet a good-looking man.
- You'll go to a famous law school.
- You'll move to another city.
- You'll win a lot of money soon.

- You'll become a firefighter, but you won't like it.
- You'll get married after you finish school.
- You'll become the first woman President.
- You'll have trouble at sea.

Elizabeth

Martin

1. a. _____

    b. _____

    c. _____

2. a. _____

    b. _____

    c. _____

Jennifer

3. a. _____

    b. _____

    c. _____

2 *Choose a correct sentence to complete each of the conversations.*

- I know, I know. I'll stop tomorrow.
- I'll call you tomorrow.
- I'll do it later. I promise.

- I'll pick you up at 7:00.
- I'll get some later.

1. A: The movie begins at 8:00.

B: _____

2. A: We're out of milk.

B: _____

3. A: I really had a nice time tonight, George.

B: Me too. _____

4. A: Danny, did you finish your homework?

B: _____

3 *Read the sentences. Then look at the pictures and write the correct sentence in each bubble.*

- Will you do the dishes? I have to study.
- Will you get some sugar on your way home tonight?

- Will you hold her for a minute?
- Will you open this for me?

GRAMMAR BOX

Will

The contraction of *will* is *'ll;* the negative form is *will not* (*won't*).

Notice how questions are formed.

> The movie **will** be over at 10:00.
> **Will** the movie   be over at 10:00?
> What time **will** the movie   be over?
> It **won't** be over until 10:00.

Use *will* for:

1. requests: **Will** you give me the newspaper when you're through?
                  Will you please not smoke?

2. promises: **I'll** give you the money when I get home.
                  Tony **won't** hire anyone until he talks to you.

3. predictions: It **will** be sunny and warm tomorrow.
                  Many experts say that the problem of world hunger **won't** be
                  solved in this century.

---

4 *Write requests, promises, and predictions with the words in parentheses. Use a form of* **will** *in all your answers.*

1. A customer is talking to an employee at a shoe-repair shop.

   A: When can I pick up my shoes?

   B: _____ They'll be ready at 4:30 this afternoon. _____
                promise: (be ready at 4:30 this afternoon)

2. A man is talking to his wife on the phone.

   A: I forgot to get milk. Will you get some on your way home?
                           request: (get some on your way home)

   B: Sure.

3. A man is talking to his wife on the phone.

A: Hi, Marge. This is Dan. I have a lot of work tonight, so _____

_____
    prediction: (probably be late for dinner)

B: That's OK. _____
                        request: (get some sugar on your way home)

A: Sure.

4. Two people are talking one morning at work.

A: Let's go to a movie tonight.

B: Good idea! _____ ,
                    promise: (meet you here after work)

and we can decide what to see.

A: Great!

5. Two university students are talking.

A: When are you going to finish your studies?

B: Oh, _____
                prediction: (probably finish in 1995 or 1996)

6. A woman and her boyfriend are talking.

A: What time are you leaving tomorrow?

B: At 2:30. _____
                    request: (take me to the airport)

A: Sorry, I can't. I have to teach from 2:00 to 4:00.

7. A husband and wife are talking.

A: The house is really a mess.

B: I know. _____
                    promise: (clean the bathroom and kitchen tomorrow)

A: OK. And _____
                    promise: (do the laundry tonight)

8. Two friends are talking.

A: I'm still looking for work.

B: Cheer up! _____
                    prediction: (find a job soon)

9. A woman is talking to her son. The son is driving.

A: Don't drive so fast. _____
prediction: (have an accident)

B: OK, OK. _____
promise: (slow down)

10. A woman is talking to her daughter.

A: I have a terrible headache. _____
request: (get me some aspirin)

B: Sure. _____
promise: (go in a minute)

Now you're ready for the computer. When you finish at the computer, go to the next exercise.

5 *Look at the pictures. Then write sentences about the people, telling what you think their future will be. You may want to write sentences like these:*

I think Jeremy will become a lawyer.
Marybel probably won't go to college.
Jacquelyn will start her own computer company.

Jacquelyn

1. _____

_____

_____

Jeremy

2. _____
   _____
   _____
   _____

Marybel

3. _____
   _____
   _____
   _____

6 *Write sentences predicting your own future. You can write sentences like the examples in Exercise 5. You can also use* **I hope.** *Use* **will** *in your affirmative sentences and* **won't** *in your negative sentences.*

1. _____

2. _____

3. _____

4. _____

5. _____

6. _____

7 *On January 1, many people make New Year's resolutions. This means they promise to do or not to do certain things during the coming year. Look at the examples. Then write New Year's resolutions for yourself.*

I'll start a new diet.
I won't lose my temper.
I'll stop smoking.
I won't complain about my job.

1. _____

2. _____

3. _____

4. _____

5. _____

1 *Look at the pictures. Then complete the sentences on the next page. There is more than one possible answer.*

van

pick-up truck

hatchback

sportscar

jeep

tricycle

Martha

Lydia

Bradley

Davy

Janie

1. I think Lydia should get the _____

2. Bradley should have the _____

3. Martha should have the _____

4. I think Davy should get the _____

5. Janie should have the _____

2 Use "I'd rather" or "I'd prefer" to answer these questions.

1. Where would you rather go on vacation, to Hawaii or to Alaska? _____

_____

2. Which course would you prefer to take, art history or biology? _____

_____

3. What would you rather have for dinner, a hamburger or roast chicken with a salad?

_____

4. Would you rather live in Canada or in Spain? _____

_____

5 Would you prefer a sportscar or a van? _____

_____

6. Would you rather see a Clint Eastwood movie or a comedy with Bette Midler?

_____

3 *Look at the menu. Then complete the conversation. Pretend that you are A, and that B and C are two friends having dinner with you.*

— Appetizers —	— Entrees —	— Desserts —
French Onion Soup Corn and Crab Soup Fried Oysters Spinach Salad	Barbecued Beef Ribs Roast Chicken Pork Chops with Apple Sauce New York Strip Steak Grilled Lamb Chops Blackened Redfish (All of the above are served with salad and baked potato.)	Warm Apple Pie with Ice Cream Pecan Pie Ice Cream Sundae Chocolate, Strawberry, Pineapple Chocolate Cake

WAITER: Are you ready to order?

    A: Yes. I'd like _____

WAITER: Would you like an appetizer?

    A: _____

WAITER: And you? What would you like?

    B: I'll have _____, and I'd like _____ too.

    C: I'll try _____ for an entree.

WAITER: And for dessert?

    B: _____

    C: I'd like _____

WAITER: Is that all?

    A: No. I'd like _____ too.

GRAMMAR BOX

Should and *Would*

Like *can* and *will*, the modals *should* and *would* do not change in form.

1. Use *should* + verb for advice:

   You should go to sleep early if you want to do well on the test tomorrow.
   You shouldn't buy that dress if it doesn't fit.

2. Use *would like* + *to* + verb or *would like* + noun to express desire:

   I'd like to go out tonight. Would you like to go to the movies?
   I'd like some cream for my tea.

3. Use *would rather* + verb to express preference.

   Would you rather have steak or lobster for dinner?
   I'd rather have lobster, thank you.

4. Use *would prefer* + *to* + verb or *would prefer* + noun to express preference:

   Would you prefer to have steak or lobster for dinner?
   I'd prefer to have lobster, thank you.

   Would you prefer steak or lobster for dinner?
   I'd prefer steak, thank you.

4 *Look at the pictures and complete the sentences using* **would rather** *or* **would prefer.**

1. Ann is a reporter for the *Barker News*, but ___ she'd rather work ___
   ___ for the Kansas City Star. ___

2. Amy goes to City College in Kansas City, but _____

_____

_____

3. Bob flies from Kansas City to New York, but _____

_____

_____

4. Rick has a bicycle, but _____

_____

_____

5. Ann lives in Barker, but _____

_____

_____

5 *Imagine that you are going to Paris. Write sentences telling what you would like or love to do there. You may want to use some of the ideas in the box.*

take a boat on the Seine	walk along the Champs Elysée
go to the top of the Eiffel Tower	visit the sewers
go shopping	drink champagne
eat frog legs	go to some museums
visit Notre Dame	eat in a famous French restaurant

1. I'd love to eat in a famous French restaurant.

2. _____

3. _____

4. _____

5. _____

6. _____

6 *Pretend that people are telling you about their problems. Make sentences giving them advice. You may want to use the phrases in the box.*

spend more time studying	lie down for a while
give it some plant food	talk to your boss
look for a house in the suburbs	call her and apologize

1. **A:** I have a headache.

   B: You should lie down for a while.

2. **A:** I had a terrible fight with my girlfriend last night, and I said some awful things to her.

   B: _____

3. **A:** My grades were awful this term. My parents are going to kill me.

   B: _____

4. A: I'm really unhappy at work. I'm the only one who does any work. Everyone else just sits around and talks.

B: _____

5. A: I don't know what's wrong with my plant. It really looks sick.

B: _____

6. A: My family and I don't like living in the city.

B: _____

7 *Look at the pictures and make a choice. Then write sentences with* **would rather** *or* **would prefer (to).**

1. I'd rather live in
San Francisco.

2. _____

3. _____

4. _____

8 *Imagine that you are going on vacation. Write a short paragraph telling what you would like to see, do, eat, and so on.*

I'd like to go to _____ on my next vacation because _____

_____

_____

_____

_____

_____

_____

_____

_____

_____

1 *Bentley Morris was murdered last night. The police know that he died at about 10:00 p.m. Nine people were in the house when he died. The police inspector asked them what they were doing at 10:00, and he wrote down their answers. Look at the picture and read the answers. Then try to figure out who committed the murder.*

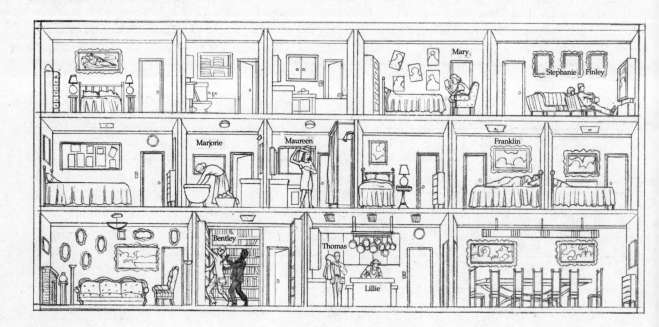

Suspects said they were doing the following at the time of the murder:

1. Mary, one of the maids, was reading in her bedroom.
2. Stephanie, Bentley's younger sister, and Finley, his brother, were watching TV in the TV room.
3. Franklin, Stephanie's husband, was sleeping.
4. Thomas, the butler, and Lillie, the other maid, were in the kitchen. Thomas was polishing the silver, and Lillie was making out a shopping list.
5. Maureen, Bentley's wife, was taking a shower.
6. Marjorie, Maureen's friend, was washing out some clothes in one of the second-floor bathrooms.
7. Jeffrey, Bentley's younger brother, was building a fire in the living room.

Who is lying? Who killed Bentley? _____

2 *Look at the picture. Then use the phrases in the box to complete the paragraph.*

were sitting	were swimming	was making
was sitting	were playing cards	were building a fire

Rick and Amy met some friends at Lone Star Lake for a picnic. When they got

there, Harry and Sally _____ 1 . Linda and Pete _____ 2 , and

Molly _____ 3 the hamburgers. Belinda and Richard _____ 4 ,

and Rafael _____ 5 next to them playing his guitar. Gary and Nellie

_____ 6 at the end of the deck fishing. Amy parked the car, and she and

Rick carried the cooler over to the picnic table.

GRAMMAR BOX

Past Progressive

1. Use *was/were* + verb-*ing* to form the past progressive.

When I got to the club, José was playing tennis, and Joel and Odette were swimming.

2. The past progressive shows an action that was taking place when another action (usually in the simple past) took place. It almost always occurs in sentences with another verb in the simple past. If the other past action is not actually stated in the sentence, it is almost always implied.

I was taking a walk when it started to rain.

I woke up early yesterday. It was a beautiful day. The sun was shining, birds were singing, and the wind was blowing gently.

3. Verbs such as *know, believe, have* (to show possession), and *be* are rarely used in the progressive.

Notice how questions are formed:

What were you   doing when I called?
     Were you   watching TV?
       I wasn't doing anything.
       I was   waiting for you to call.

---

3 *A reporter is talking to some people who experienced the 1985 earthquake in Mexico City. Complete the interview with the words in parentheses. Use the correct past or past-progressive form of the verb.*

INTERVIEWER: So _____ *you were* _____ in Mexico City during the big
                              (you / be)

               earthquake of 1985.

CARMEN: That's right. It was awful.

INTERVIEWER: What were you doing when _____?
                                          (1. the earthquake/hit)

CARMEN: Well, _____ a little before 7:00
(2. it / start)

in the morning, and _____.
(3. I / sleep)

_____ and _____
(4. I / wake up)   (5. I / realize)

that _____. _____
(6. everything / move)   (7. the ceiling lamps / swing)

back and forth, _____,
(8. my bed / shake)

_____, and
(9. the curtains / move)

_____ as it opened and closed.
(10. one of the windows / bang)

INTERVIEWER: How long _____?
(11. it / last)

CARMEN: _____ about two minutes, but I
(12. it / last)

thought it was two years.

INTERVIEWER: What _____?
(13. you / do)

CARMEN: _____ out of bed, and
(14. I / jump)

_____ outdoors.
(15. I / run)

INTERVIEWER: _____ smart.
(16. that / be)

CARMEN: Yes. _____ full of people.
(17. the streets / be)

INTERVIEWER: What were they doing?

CARMEN: _____ in the middle of the street, terrified.
(18. some / just / stand)

_____ up and down and screaming.
(19. others / run)

INTERVIEWER: _____?
(20. your building / fall)

CARMEN: No. _____ lucky.
(21. I / be)

Now the interviewer interviews other people.

INTERVIEWER: What ___*were you doing*___ when
(you / do)

_____?
(22. the earthquake / hit)

MARCOS: _____ to work.
(23. I / drive)

41

INTERVIEWER: And you, Mrs. Hernández?

MRS. HERNANDEZ: _____ breakfast for my son. He had
(24. I / make)

an 8:00 class at the university. _____
(25. I / be)

terrified. _____ off the stove.
(26. all the pots / fall)

_Now you're ready for the computer. When you finish at the computer, go to the next
exercise._

4 _This picture was taken at a New Year's Eve party last year just as the clock was
striking midnight. Write sentences about what the people were doing when the
clock struck 12:00._

1. Danny _____ *was playing the piano.* _____

2. Jeff _____

3. Mario and Daisy _____

4. Philip _____

5. Ralph and Marsha _____

6. Hank _____

7. Debbie _____

8. Peggy _____

9. Martin _____

5 *Write one or two paragraphs with the simple past and the past progressive. You can begin like this:*

When I got to class yesterday,
When I got to work last week,
When I came down to breakfast this morning,
When I got up this morning,

_____

_____

_____

_____

_____

_____

_____

_____

_____

_____

1 Look at the vocabulary box.

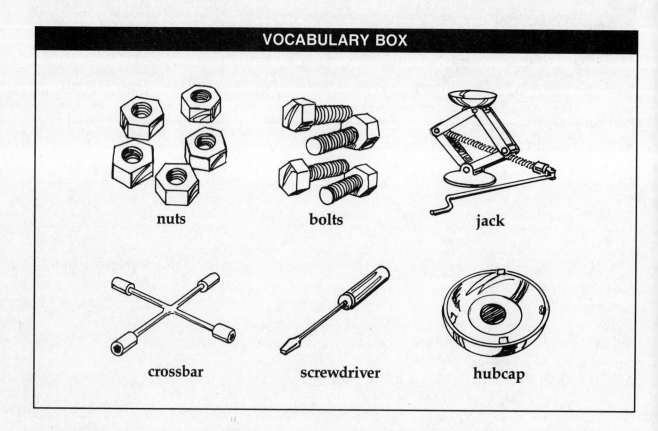

VOCABULARY BOX

nuts

bolts

jack

crossbar

screwdriver

hubcap

Read the instructions for fixing a flat tire. Then look at the pictures here and on the following page. Write the correct sentence under each picture.

- Take the nuts off the bolts and take off the tire.
- Don't tighten the nuts until the tire is touching the ground.
- Stop the car as soon as you can.
- Don't move the car while it is in this position.
- Jack up the car.
- Use the jack to lower the car.
- When you finish tightening the nuts, put the hubcap back on.
- Put the new tire on and screw in the nuts with your hand only.
- Unscrew all the nuts before you jack up the car.
- Use a screwdriver to take off the hubcap.

1. <u>Stop the car as soon</u>
   <u>as you can.</u>

2. _____

3. _____

4. _____

5. _____

6. _____

7. _____

8. _____

9. _____   10. _____

_____   _____

GRAMMAR BOX

Adverbial Time Clauses

Adverbial time clauses show the time relationship between two verbs—the verb in the adverbial clause and the verb in the independent clause. They begin with words like *after, before, when, while, until,* and *as soon as.* Notice that when an adverbial clause comes at the beginning of a sentence, it is followed by a comma.

after
After we eat, we'll wash the dishes.
We'll wash the dishes after we eat.
After we ate, we washed the dishes.
We washed the dishes after we ate.

before
Before he comes, I'll leave.
I'll leave before he comes.
Before he came, I left.
I left before he came.

when
When he arrives, I'll call you.
I'll call you when he arrives.
When he arrived, I called you.
I called you when he arrived.

while
While Kate's studying, I'll cook.
I'll cook while Kate's studying.
While Kate studied, I cooked.
I cooked while Kate studied.

until
Until evening, it will be hot.
It will be hot until evening.
Until evening, it was hot.
It was hot until evening.

as soon as
As soon as I get home, I'll call you.
I'll call you as soon as I get home.
As soon as I got home, I called you.
I called you as soon as I got home.

Note: When an adverbial clause comes at the beginning of a sentence, it is followed by a comma.

2 *Use one clause from each column to make a sentence that goes with each picture.*
Then write the sentence under the appropriate picture.

Don't make noise   after you do your homework.
Look both ways   before you come into the house.
Don't talk   while my friends are here.
You can watch TV   when you have food in your mouth.
Wipe your feet   before you cross the street.
You can't go out and play   as soon as you finish playing.
Be sure you put away your toys until you clean your room.
Call me   when you're ready to come home.

1. _Don't make noise while_
   my friends are here.

2. _____

3. _____
   _____

Do your homework first.

4. _____
   _____

5. _____

6. _____

7. _____

8. _____

3 *What are some things your parents told you to do or not to do? Use one of these words in each of your sentences:* **when, after, before, while, as soon as, until.**

1. _____ Don't watch TV while you're studying. _____

2. _____

3. _____

4. _____

5. _____

6. _____

4 *Complete this recipe with one of these adverbs:* **when, while, before, until, after.**

Put the chocolate chips in a blender. If you are using chocolate squares, cut the chocolate in small pieces _____ you put it in the blender. Add all other
1
ingredients except the milk. _____ you add the milk, put it in a
2
saucepan and heat it _____ it is very hot, but not boiling.
3
_____ the milk is hot, pour it over the chocolate in the blender and
4
blend. Blend _____ all the ingredients are smooth. Don't leave
5
the blender _____ it is running. _____ you finish blending,
6   7
pour the mixture into six small dessert dishes or one large mold. Put in the refrigerator
and chill. _____ the mousse is firm, serve with whipped cream.
8

5 *Look at the pictures. Then rewrite the instructions by combining the sentences that are under each picture. Use* **when, before, after, while** *or* **until** *in each new sentence. You may use the adverbial clause either as the first or the second clause in your sentences. Write your sentences on the next page.*

1. Turn the computer on.
   Put the disk in the disk drive.

2. Put the disk in.
   Be sure the door to the disk drive
   is closed.

3. You see this on the screen:
   ENTER TIME and *ENTER DATE.*
   Type in the date and the time.

4. Then wait.
   The program loads.

5. Don't start typing.
   You see this on the screen: *NOW BEGIN.*

1. _____ Turn the computer on before you put the disk
_____ in the disk drive.

2. _____

_____

3. _____

_____

4. _____

_____

5. _____

_____

Now you're ready for the computer. When you finish at the computer, go on to the next exercise.

6 *Combine the sentences with the word in parentheses. Then use the new sentences to complete Ann's note.*

1. Finish eating breakfast. Put your dishes in the dishwasher and turn it on. (after)
2. Please take out the garbage. Go to school. (before)
3. Get home from school. Please take the roast out of the refrigerator and put it in the oven at 350 degrees. (when)
4. It can cook. I get home at 6:00. (until)

_____Rick_____,

_____, _____
    1
_____, _____.

___Then___, _____
                                   2
_____. I'm going to

get home late, so _____, _____
                 3
_____. _____

_____.
                       4
Thanks. See you tonight.

                                   _____Mom_____

Now you're ready for the computer. When you finish at the computer, go to the next exercise.

7 *Complete these sentences with information about yourself.*

1. I usually don't _____ until _____
_____

2. I like to _____ before _____
_____

3. Before _____, I always _____
_____

4. I often _____ after _____
_____

5. I never _____ while _____
_____

6. As soon as _____, I _____
_____

Now answer these questions. Use complete sentences.

1. Do you ever do something else while you watch TV?
_____

2. What do you like to do when you go on vacation?
_____

3. What did you do yesterday before you ate breakfast?
_____

4. What are you going to do today after you finish this exercise?
_____

5. Is there anything you like to do as soon as you get home from school or work?
_____

1 *Use the clauses in the box to complete the conversations.*

some might come early	we might not have enough
My boss might call	It might rain

1. _____,

and I don't want to talk to her.

2. It's really cloudy.

_____.

3. I know, but _____

4. I know, but _____

2 *Rick's history teacher wrote two lists on the blackboard the first day of class. Read the phrases. Then complete the lists by writing the phrases in the correct column.*

- turn in any homework papers late
- get to class on time
- participate in every class
- do all the homework assignments

- get below 90 on any test
- give 3 short reports to the class
- miss any classes
- write a 5-page paper

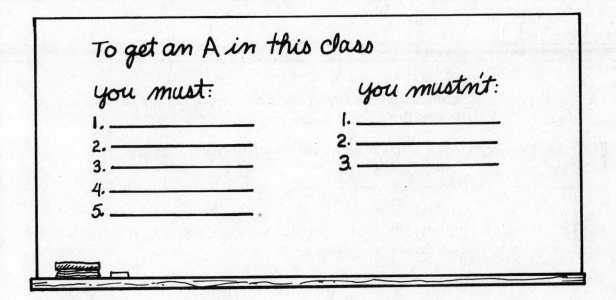

To get an A in this class

you must:
1. _____
2. _____
3. _____
4. _____
5. _____

you mustn't:
1. _____
2. _____
3. _____

3 *Use one of the two responses in the box to complete each pair of conversations.*

1. **A:** Eliza just rewired my whole kitchen and fixed the light in my bedroom.

   B: _She must know a lot about electrical wiring._

   A: I can't get the lights in my kitchen to work.

   B: Ask Jane to look at them. _Her father is an electrician so_ _____

   She must know a lot about electrical wiring.
   She might know something about electrical wiring.

2. A: Mike has about 50 plants in his apartment.

B: _____

A: What can I get Bill for his birthday?

B: _____

> He might like a plant.
> He must really like plants.

3. A: Some people are coming over to my house tomorrow night and I want to give them something to eat. But I don't even know how to boil water.

B: I don't either. But Frank has lived alone for a few years. _____

_____

A: Robert is cooking dinner for twelve people tomorrow night. He's going to make five different French dishes!

B: _____

> He might know how to cook.
> He must be a good cook.

4. A: I'd really like some fresh strawberries for dinner.

B: Franklin Supermarket has over 50 different kinds of fruit. _____

_____

A: I'd really like some fresh strawberries for dinner.

B: The little grocery store on the corner sometimes has fresh fruit. _____

_____

> They might have fresh strawberries.
> They must have fresh strawberries.

Must and *Might*

1. Use *must* for:

    a. obligation: The wheel on Tommy's bicycle is loose. We must tighten it. He mustn't ride his bike until that wheel is fixed.

    b. probability: Pamela always dresses beautifully. She must spend most of her salary on clothes, and she must not have much left for her rent and other expenses.

2. Use *might* for possibility: Mr. and Mrs. Soto might go dancing on Friday night; they don't know for sure yet because the babysitter might not be able to come.

Note: The contraction *mustn't* is almost never used for probability; use the full form (*must not*) instead.

Might not is never contracted.

4 Look at the pictures. Then complete the conversations using **might** and the word in parentheses.

1. **A:** Where are the Dalys going on their vacation this year?

   B: Well, (*go*) _____

   _____,

   or _____

   _____

2. **A:** What's Amy going to take this semester?

   B: I'm not sure. (*take*)

   _____

   _____,

   or _____

   _____

3. A: What kind of car is Ann going

to get?

B: I don't know. (*get*) _____

_____,

or _____

_____

_____

4. A: Who's Rick going to take to the

high school dance on Saturday?

B: Who knows? (*invite*) _____

_____,

or _____

_____

_____

5 *Complete the sentences with* **might** *or* **must.**

1. Dick has been smoking for years, and now he is having trouble breathing. He

_____ stop smoking.

2. Linda smokes ten cigarettes a day. She knows it isn't good for her, so she

_____ stop smoking.

3. Gail took four exams in English this semester, and she failed two of them. She

_____ fail the course.

4. Howard is a senior in college, and he is failing two of his courses. He

_____ pass those courses, or he won't graduate this year.

5. In some Moslem countries, women cover most of their bodies. Tourists

_____ (*neg.*) wear shorts or short dresses in these countries.

6. I _____ (*neg.*) not see you at the picnic tomorrow because I think I have

to work later in the afternoon.

Now you're ready for the computer. When you finish at the computer, go to the next exercise.

6 *Answer these questions. Use* **might** *in your answers.*

1. Pretend you are going to buy a new car. What car do you think you'll buy? _____

_____

2. What do you think you'll do after school (or after work) tomorrow? _____

_____

3. Where do you think you'll go on your next vacation? _____

_____

4. What do you think you'll be doing ten years from now? _____

_____

7 *Write sentences with* **might** *or* **must** *and the words in parentheses.*

1. Amy always makes the best grades in class. (*very smart*) _____

_____

2. Bob learned to fly when he was 22, and he still flies almost every day. (*really like
to fly*) _____

3. The Dalys are giving their guests snails for dinner tonight, but I don't think that's
a very good idea. (*like snails, neg.*) _____

4. Bob's boss, Mr. Gerber, just bought a $50,000 car and a new house. (*have a lot of money*) _____

5. Rick just told me he wants to learn to play the guitar. (*take guitar lessons next year*)

_____

6. Bob would prefer to work for a bigger airline. (*leave Skyway Airlines*) _____

_____

7. A friend of Amy's doesn't have a job and lives in her camper. (*have much money, neg.*)

_____

8. Amy started working with computers over five years ago. She works with them every day now. (*know a lot about them*) _____

_____

8 *Read these situations. Think about each one and write a sentence using **must** or **might**. Sometimes either choice is correct.*

1. My cat just sits in the corner all day. She doesn't eat, and she looks awful.

_____She must be sick._____

2. I called Roger three times yesterday and four times today, but no one answered.

_____

3. Linda hasn't studied all week. She has a test tomorrow. _____

_____

4. Jerry ordered a big steak for dinner, but he isn't eating it. _____

_____

5. The Allens just won $1,000,000. _____

_____

1 *Look at the pictures of some of the things that Amy does. Then write sentences with the phrases in the box. Begin each sentence with* **She enjoys** *... or* **She can't stand** *....*

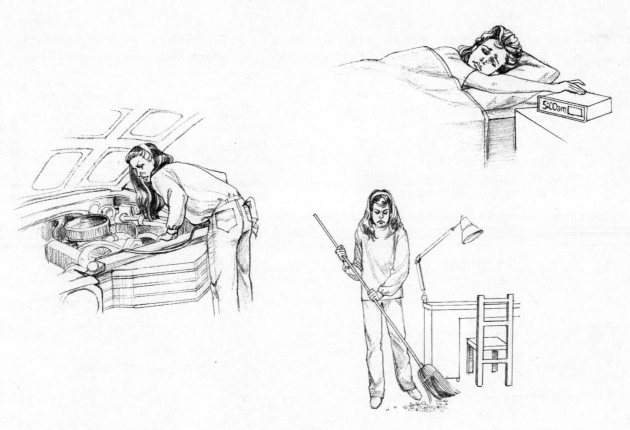

1. _She can't stand getting up early._
   (getting up early)

2. _____
   (playing the piano)

3. _____
   (dancing)

4. _____
   (cleaning her room)

5. _____
   (eating out with friends)

6. _____
   (fixing her car)

7. _____
   (working in the library)

8. _____
   (taking out the garbage)

9. _____
   (lying in the sun)

10. _____
    (playing baseball)

2 *Look again at the pictures on pages 62 and 63. Then use one of the phrases in each pair to write sentences about what you think Amy plans, intends, or would like to do.*

change jobs / keep her job	ask Rick to take out the garbage /
get up early every day /	take the garbage out herself
get up late every day	eat out more often / cook at home
avoid dancing whenever possible /	take piano lessons / quit piano
go dancing twice a week	lessons

1. _____ She plans to change jobs. _____

2. _____

3. _____

4. _____

5. _____

6. _____

3 *Read the sentences. Then look at the pictures and write the correct sentence under each picture.*

- Do not use while smoking.
- Remove from can and refrigerate.

- Take only after eating.
- Shake before opening.

1. _____ 2. _____

_____ _____

3. _____

    _____

4. _____

    _____

GRAMMAR BOX

Verbs Followed by Gerunds or Infinitives

1. Use an infinitive (*to* + verb) following some verbs: *agree, decide, expect, hope, intend, learn, would like/love, need, plan, promise, refuse, want.*

    Why did you decide to become an actress? Do you hope to be famous?
    I plan to work hard and I refuse to give up. In the meantime, I'll need to borrow some money from you.

2. Use a gerund (verb + *ing*) following other verbs: *enjoy, finish, keep, stop.*

    Do you enjoy watching TV?
    When you finish talking, I hope you'll let me say something.
    Why do the children keep pulling the dog's tail?
    Gary's doctor told him that he must stop smoking.

3. Use a gerund following certain verb phrases (verb + preposition); prepositions are almost always followed by gerunds, not by infinitives: *be tired of, be used to, feel like, go on, insist on, look forward to, talk/ask/wonder about; before, after, while.*

    The neighbors must be tired of hearing you play the drums.
    Lila always had a roommate, so she isn't used to living alone.
    My brother is looking forward to starting college.
    At this company, the employees must sign out before leaving.

4. Some verbs can be followed by either a gerund or an infinitive: *begin, hate, like, love, prefer, remember, can't stand, start, try.*

    It began to rain at noon.   It began raining at noon.
    He likes to talk on the phone.   He likes talking on the phone.
    I hate to pay bills.   I hate paying bills.

4 *This is an article from the **Barker News**. Complete the article with the correct forms of the verbs. In some cases, both answers are possible.*

Neighbors at War

PLATTSVILLE, IOWA—A year ago Mr. and Mrs. Rogers

decided _____ a fence around their
(1. to build / building)

yard. "We wanted _____ up a fence
(2. to put / putting)

because we like _____ in the sun, and
(3. to lie / lying)

the Parsons, our neighbors, kept _____
(4. to look / looking)

at us," said Mrs. Rogers. "We just got tired of their

_____ at us, so we decided _____
(5. to stare / staring)   (6. to do / doing)

something about it. After _____ the
(7. to build / building)

fence, we really looked forward _____
(8. to live / to living)

in peace and privacy. And then, suddenly, the Parsons

started _____ their garbage over the
(9. to dump / dumping)

fence into our yard! Can you believe it? We asked them

to stop, but they keep _____ it. I guess
(10. to do / doing)

they're angry because of the fence and they enjoy

_____ us."
(11. to bother / bothering)

"It's all lies," say the Parsons. "Of course, they didn't

ask us about _____ a fence. They just
(12. to build / building)

felt like _____ one and so they did. It
(13. to build / building)

ruined our view. When they started _____
(14. to build / building)

it, we asked them to stop, but they refused

_____. Of course, we're angry, but we
(15. to listen / listening)

are NOT throwing anything in their yard. They insist

on _____ us. They're just crazy and we
(16. to accuse / accusing)

intend _____ to court about this. And
(17. to go / going)

we expect _____."
(18. to win / winning)

Now you're ready for the computer. When you finish at the computer, go to the next exercise.

5 *Ann Daly is talking to a friend at work. Complete the conversation with the correct infinitive or the gerund forms of the verbs in parentheses.*

ANN: What are you planning _____ on your vacation?
(1. do)

STEVE: I want _____ as far away from this newspaper as I can. I'd love
(2. go)

_____ to Hawaii. I intend _____ on the beach and
(3. go)   (4. lie)

do nothing.

ANN: Really? Do you really enjoy _____ on the beach?
(5. lie)

STEVE: Yes! Don't you?

ANN: Not really. I can't stand _____ sand all over me, and I hate
(6. get)

_____ all hot and sticky and _____ the sun in my eyes.
(7. get)   (8. have)

I'd much prefer _____ to Alaska.
(9. go)

STEVE: That's funny. My wife was talking about _____ to Alaska last year.
(10. go)

But she was thinking about _____ in the summer.
(11. go)

ANN: There are too many mosquitoes in the summer.

STEVE: That's true. Well, I'm looking forward to _____ for a week, no
(12. sleep)

matter where I go. I'm exhausted from _____ to bed at midnight
(13. go)

and _____ up at 5:00 every day.
(14. get)

ANN: I know what you mean.

6 *Complete these sentences with either an infinitive or a gerund.*

1. I really enjoy _____

2. I love _____

3. I can't stand _____

4. I sometimes _____ while _____

5. I refuse _____

6. I always _____ before _____

7. Every morning I look forward to _____

1 *Read the list of chores that Ann left for Rick and Amy.*

Rick	Amy	Both
take out the garbage	wash my car	clean bathroom
cut grass	water plants	throw out old newspapers
fix living room lamp	clean stove	in basement
nail down living room rug	mop kitchen	do laundry
take the bicycle to the	floor	clean your bedrooms
basement		

Now look at the picture and cross out the incorrect sentence.

1. Rick has already cut the grass.
   ~~Rick hasn't cut the grass yet.~~

2. He's already fixed the lamp in the living room.
   He hasn't fixed the lamp in the living room yet.

3. He's already taken out the garbage.
   He hasn't taken out the garbage yet either.

4. Amy has already cleaned the bathroom.
   Amy hasn't cleaned the bathroom yet.

5. She's already washed Ann's car and cleaned the stove.
   She hasn't washed Ann's car yet, and she hasn't cleaned the stove yet either.

6. Both Amy and Rick have already cleaned their bedrooms.
   Neither Amy nor Rick has cleaned their bedrooms yet.

7. They've already thrown out the old newspapers.
   They haven't thrown out the old newspapers yet.

8. They've done the laundry too.
   They haven't done the laundry yet either.

Now use the correct sentences on this page to complete this paragraph about what Amy and Rick have already done and what they haven't done yet.

It's 2:30 in the afternoon. _____ Rick has already cut _____
___ the grass ___, but _____
2
_____, and he hasn't _____
3
_____ . _____
4
_____, but _____
5
_____ . _____
_____, but
6
_____
7
_____ either.
8

69

2

Answer these questions about the picture in Exercise 1. Use these short answers:
Yes, he has. / No, he hasn't. / Yes, she has. / No, she hasn't. / Yes, they have. / No, they haven't.

1. Have Amy and Rick cleaned the bathroom yet? ___No they haven't.___

2. Has Amy mopped the kitchen floor yet? _____

3. Has Rick nailed down the living room rug yet? _____

4. Has he taken the bicycles to the basement yet? _____

3

Answer these questions about yourself. Use **Yes, I have.** *or* **No, I haven't.**

1. Have you graduated from high school yet? _____

2. Have you ever run in a race? _____

3. Have you ever written a novel? _____

4. Have you ever flown an airplane? _____

5. Have you ever flown in an airplane? _____

6. Have you ever ridden a camel? _____

7. Have you ever ridden a horse? _____

8. Have you ever been to Australia? _____

Present Perfect

1. Use *have/has* + past participle to form the present perfect tense.

2. Regular past participles are formed by adding *-ed* or *-d* to the simple form of the verb: play → played; live → lived. Study these irregular forms:

be	been	make	made
drive	driven	meet	met
eat	eaten	ride	ridden
fly	flown	run	run
get	gotten	see	seen
give	given	spend	spent
go	gone	take	taken
have	had	think	thought
know	known	win	won
leave	left	write	written

3. The present perfect expresses the idea that something happened (or didn't happen) at an indefinite time in the past. *Yet, already, ever,* and *never* are often used when the present perfect has this meaning.

yet	Have you seen *Hamlet* yet? No, I haven't seen it yet.	*Yet* is used with questions and in the negative.
already	I've already seen that play.	
ever	Have you ever flown a plane?	When used with the present perfect, *ever* = at any time before the present.
never	I've never flown a plane.	When used with the present perfect, *never* = at no time before the present.

4. If you know the specific time that something happened, use the simple past tense.

Did you see the dance special last night?	No, I watched a news program instead.

4 *Betty and Shirley are in Greece. Read the list of things they plan to do.*

1. go to the Acropolis in Athens
2. eat at the Three Brothers Restaurant
3. go to the archeological museum
4. visit the ruins at Mycenae
5. See a play in the theater at Epidaurus
6. see the labyrinth at Knossos
7. go to the ruins at Delphi
8. go to Mount Olympus

Now look at the pictures. Betty's pictures show the places they have already seen. Look at the list again and write sentences about where the girls have already been and where they haven't been yet.

Shirley and me at the Acropolis

Having dinner at the Three Brothers Restaurant

Shirley in front of the museum

Shirley and me in the theater at Epidaurus

1.   They've already gone to the Acropolis in Athens.

2. _____

3. _____

4. <u>They haven't visited the ruins at Mycenae yet.</u>

5. _____

6. _____

7. _____

8. _____

5 *Write questions with the words in parentheses. Then look again at the pictures in Exercise 4 and answer the questions. Use short answers:* **Yes, they have,** *or* **No, they haven't.**

1. <u>Have Betty and Shirley seen a Greek temple yet?</u>
(Betty and Shirley / see / a Greek temple / yet)

   <u>Yes, they have.</u>

2. _____
(they be / to any museums / yet)

   _____

3. _____
(they / eat / Greek food / yet)

   _____

4. _____
(they / go / to Crete to see Knossos / yet)

   _____

Create questions with the words in parentheses. Then answer these questions about yourself. Use short answers: **Yes, I have,** *or* **No, I haven't.**

1. _____
(you / ever / be / to Greece)

   _____

2. _____
(you / ever / see / a picture of a Greek theater)

   _____

3. _____
(you / ever / see or read / a Greek play)

   _____

6 Read the examples. Then write questions that you would like to ask a friend. Use the present perfect in your questions.

Have you ever driven a motorcycle?
Have you ever won a special award or prize?
Have you ever seen the Empire State Building?

1. _____

2. _____

3. _____

4. _____

5. _____

7 Think about things that you would like to do. Then complete these sentences.

1. I've _____, but I've

   never _____.

2. I've never _____ either.

3. I've never _____, but I've

   _____.

4. I've _____ too.

Now you're ready for the computer. When you finish at the computer, go to the next exercise.

8 Ten years ago, Belinda Rogers made a list of the things she wanted to do in her life. As she did each thing on her list, she crossed it out. Write sentences about what she's already done and what she hasn't done yet.

— ~~graduate from college~~
— live in Japan
— learn Japanese
— ~~join a good architectural firm~~
— open my own architectural firm
— ~~get married~~
— ~~have 3 children~~
— ~~run in the New York Marathon~~
— write a novel
— ~~buy a house on a hill~~
— make $1,000,000
— learn to fly

1. _____She's already graduated from college._____

2. _____

3. _____

4. _____

5. _____

6. _____

7. _____

8. _____

9. _____

10. _____

11. _____

12. _____

9 *Read the example. Then write about some goals you have already accomplished and some you haven't accomplished yet.*

I've already graduated from high school, but I haven't finished college yet.

1. _____

2. _____

3. _____

4. _____

5. _____

10 *Complete the conversations with the words in parentheses. Use either the simple past or the present perfect.*

1. **A:** Where is *Danger* playing?

   B: At the Howell Theater.

   A: _____
   (you / see / it / yet)

   B: No. I hope to go tomorrow.

2. **A:** Where is *Danger* playing?

   B: It isn't playing in town anymore.

   A: Oh. _____
   (you / see / it)

   B: Yes. It was awful!

3. **A:** Is your father still visiting you?

   B: Yes. He'll be here for three more days.

   A: _____
   (you / take him / to the zoo)

   B: Not yet.

4. **A:** Is your father still here?

   B: No. He went home yesterday.

   A: _____
   (you / take him / to the zoo)

   B: No. He doesn't really like zoos.

11 *Pretend that you are on a trip. Write a postcard to a friend and tell him or her about two or three places you have already visited or seen, and two or three you haven't been to yet.*

1 Read the story about Bob Daly's mother. Then answer the questions.

Nora McKinley Daly was born in Mississippi. She came to Kansas in 1935 when she was 21 years old. She worked as a teacher for two years and then she started working as a secretary for a small newspaper in Barker. Before the end of her first year, she was a reporter as well as a secretary—probably one of the first women reporters in Kansas.

In 1939 a young man named Frank Daly moved to Barker and opened a hardware store. Nora met Frank when she interviewed him the day his store opened, July 1, 1939. In January of 1941, they got married. But Nora didn't stop working. She stayed on as a reporter and today is the editor-in-chief of the *Barker News.*

1. When was Nora Daly born? _____

2. How long has she lived in Kansas? _____

3. When did she arrive in Kansas? _____

4. How long did she work as a teacher? _____

5. When did she become a reporter? _____

6. How long have Mr. and Mrs. Daly known each other? _____

7. How long have they been married? _____

8. How long has Nora been a newspaper woman? _____

9. How long has Frank Daly lived in Barker? _____

10. How long has he had a hardware store? _____

Now write **T** *if the statement is true,* **F** *if it's false.*

1. _____ Frank Daly has lived in Barker since 1935.

2. _____ Nora Daly has lived in Barker for over 50 years.

3. _____ Frank has had a hardware store for over 50 years.

4. _____ Nora has worked at the *Barker News* for 20 years.

5. _____ Nora has worked at the *Barker News* since 1936.

6. _____ Nora and Frank have been married since 1941.

7. _____ They've been married for over 50 years.

2 Answer these questions.

1. Where do you live? _____

2. How long have you lived there? _____

3. Where do you study or work? _____

4. How long have you studied or worked there? _____

5. If you are married, how long have you been married? _____

6. If you have a girlfriend or boyfriend, how long have you known her or him? _____

   _____

7. What kind of TV do you have? _____

8. How long have you had it? _____

Simple Past vs. Present Perfect

1. In general, use the simple past when the action was completed at a specific point in the past.

   I started high school in 1987, and I finished in 1991.

   Use the present perfect when the situation began in the past and continues in the present. *For* or *since* followed by a time expression is usually used with the present perfect tense.

   I know Nora and Frank. I've known them since 1952.
   I've known them for a long time.

2. *For* is followed by a time expression that shows the duration of time.

   I've been here for three months.

3. *Since* is followed by a time expression that gives a specific moment in time.

   I've been here since January.

   Since can also be followed by a clause. The verb in this clause is almost always in the simple past tense.

   I've known him since he moved here.

3 *Complete the conversations with the correct form of the verbs in parentheses. Use either the simple past or the present perfect.*

1. **A:** How long _____ you and Mary _____ married?
        (have)   (be)

   B: Let's see. We _____ married in 1950, so that means we
                        (get)

   _____ married over 40 years. But we _____ each
   (be)   (know)

   other since 1948.

2. **A:** When _____ the Borcheks _____ to the U.S.?
               (did)   (come)

   B: They _____ before the First World War, in 1916. They
               (come)

   _____ in Chicago for about ten years and then they
   (live)

   _____ here in 1926. They _____ here
   (move)   (be)

   ever since.

3. **A:** That's a beautiful old car.

   B: Thanks. You know, I _____ this car for over 35 years. My father
                              (have)

   _____ it to me when I _____ from high school.
   (give)   (graduate)

   I _____ it ever since.
     (keep)

4. **A:** Hey, coach! What's wrong with Willie? He _____ for over
                                                   (play, *neg.*)

   a month.

   B: He _____ in the hospital since the first of the month. He
             (be)

   _____ his leg skiing.
   (break)

4 *Read the headlines and think of questions that you might ask yourself before you read each article. Then write questions with the words in parentheses.*

1. Lions Lose Again!

a. _____
(what / be / the score)

b. _____
(how many games / lose)

c. _____
(who / lose to)

d. _____
(how many games / play)

2. Girl Scouts Still in Hospital with Strange Illness

a. _____
(how / get sick)

b. _____
(how long / be / sick)

c. _____
(how long / be / in the hospital)

3. King and Queen of Spain Celebrate Wedding Anniversary

a. _____
(when / get married)

b. _____
(how long / be married)

c. _____
(how / celebrate)

4. Madonna Gets Another Gold Record

a. _____
(when / get / the gold record)

b. _____
(how many gold records / get)

c. _____
(how many records / sell / up until now)

5 *Complete the paragraphs with* **for** *or* **since.**

Tomiko, a friend of Amy's, has been in the United States _____ three years, and
                                                              1
she has been in Kansas City _____ January. When she first arrived, she stayed
                              2
in a hotel, but she has had a dormitory room at City College _____ February when
                                                              3
school started. ''I studied English in Japan _____ five years,'' said Tomiko, ''and
                                              4
then I studied it _____ two more years after I came to the States. But now I can
                  5
take regular college courses. I haven't had to study English _____ last June.''
                                                             6

1 *Look at the information about the rock star Bruce Springsteen. Then write **T** if the statement is true, **F** if it's false.*

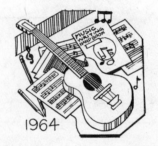

1. _____ He was born in Freehold, New Jersey.

2. _____ He's 40 years old.

3. _____ He saw Elvis Presley on television when he was eight.

4. _____ He's been writing songs since he was twelve.

5. _____ He's been playing with bands since 1964.

6. _____ He made his first record in 1972.

Now answer these questions about Bruce Springsteen.

1. When was Bruce Springsteen born? _____

2. How long ago did he see Elvis Presley for the first time? _____

3. How long has he been playing with a band? _____

4. How many years has he been writing songs? _____

5. How many years has he been making records? _____

GRAMMAR BOX

Present Perfect Progressive

1. Use *have/has been* + verb-*ing* to form the present perfect progressive.

2. The present perfect progressive shows an action that began in the past and continues into the present. It emphasizes that the action is still in progress.

I've been painting all afternoon. (I started painting earlier and am still painting.)

3. *Lately, for,* and *since* are time expressions commonly used with the present perfect progressive.

Carlos has been playing tennis {
lately.
for many years.
since 1986.

4. Verbs such as *arrive, be, believe, belong, decide, have* (to show possession), *know, like, love, start,* and *understand* are rarely used in the present perfect progressive.

5. The present perfect progressive is never used to express a repeated action when a specific number of times or repetitions is given.

She's been coming here all week.
But: She's come here four times this week.

Notice how questions are formed:

What **have** you been doing all morning?
    Have you been studying?
No, I **haven't.**
    I' **ve**   been trying to clean up this house.

2 *Look at the pictures and complete the sentences about what the Dalys have been doing lately. Use the words in parentheses.*

1. Amy __hasn't been sleeping__ and
   (not sleep)
   __she's been getting headaches__ lately.
   (get headaches)

2. Ann _____
   (work too hard)
   _____ lately.

3. Rick and Amy _____
   (not get along very well)
   _____ lately.

4. Bob _____
   (play a lot of tennis)
   _____ lately.

5. Rick _____
   (not eat very much)
   _____ lately.

Now you're ready for the computer. When you finish at the computer, go to the next exercise.

3 *Look at the information about Bob. Then write questions with the words in parentheses and answer the questions. Use the present perfect progressive when possible.*

REMEMBER:

Now Bob
- lives in Barker, Kansas.
- works for Skyways Airlines.
- is still married to Ann.
- still jogs, plays tennis, and coaches Little League baseball.

1945, BARKER KANSAS   1952   1960

1. **When was Bob born?**
   (when / born)
   In 1945.

2. _____
   (how long / live / Barker, Kansas)

3. _____
   (when / learn / to play baseball)

4. _____
   (how long / play / tennis)

5. _____
   (when / learn / to fly)

87

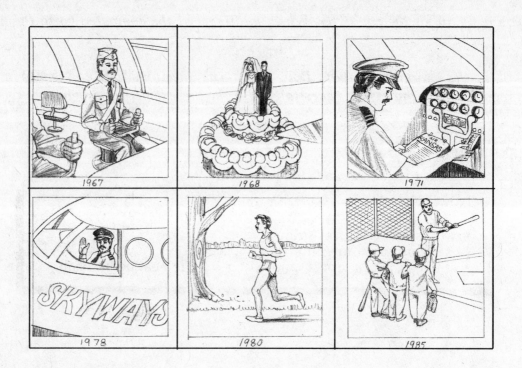

6. _____
   (how long / fly)

_____

7. _____
   (how long / be married)

_____

8. _____
   (which airline / work / for first)

_____

9. _____
   (how long / work / for them)

_____

10. _____
    (how long / work / for Skyways)

_____

11. _____
    (when / start / jogging)

_____

12. _____
    (how long / coach / Little League baseball)

_____

4 Complete the conversations with the correct form of the verbs in parentheses.

1. **A:** Can Dick play the guitar?

   B: Sure. He _____ (play) for years. Dad _____ (get) him a guitar when he _____ (be) about ten, and he _____ (play) ever since.

2. **A:** How long _____ (have) you _____ (know) Andy?

   B: I _____ (meet) him when I _____ (work) for his father last year. We _____ (date) ever since.

3. **A:** I'm really tired. I _____ (cook) all afternoon.

   B: _____ you _____ (finish, *neg.*) yet?

   A: Yes, and I _____ already _____ (set) the table too.

4. **A:** I'm sorry I'm late.

   B: That's OK. We _____ (wait, *neg.*) long.

   A: _____ you _____ (order) yet?

   B: No. We _____ (talk).

5 Pretend you are writing to a friend you haven't seen for a long time. Write a paragraph of three or four sentences saying what you did last year. Then write another paragraph of about three or four sentences saying what you've been doing lately.

_____

_____

_____

_____

_____

_____

1 *After Ann and Bob got married, they lived in a small one-room apartment. Read the apartment rules. Then complete the sentences with* **could** *or* **couldn't.**

APARTMENT RULES
—Do not keep pets in the apartment.
—Do not use extra heaters.
—Cook only in kitchenette.
—Do not hang wet laundry in bedroom.
—Do not paint walls.
—Hang pictures with picture hooks. Do not use nails.
—Do not put plants outside of windows.
—Use only 60-watt light bulbs.
—Do not put garbage in halls or out in front of building.

1. They _____ have pets.

2. They _____ use extra heaters when it was very cold.

3. They _____ cook only in the kitchenette.

4. They _____ do the laundry, but they _____ hang anything

   in the bedroom to dry.

5. The walls were really dirty, but they _____ paint them.

6. They _____ hang pictures, but they _____ use nails to

   hang them.

7. They _____ put any plants outside the windows.

8. They _____ change the bulbs in the lamps, but they _____

   use 100-watt bulbs.

9. They _____ put garbage out in front of the building.

Now answer these questions. Use **Yes, they could** *or* **No, they couldn't.**

1. Could Ann and Bob have a cat in their first apartment?

   _____

2. Could they cook? _____

3. Could they clean the walls? _____

4. Could they put up posters with nails? _____

5. Could they have plants? _____

6. Could they change the light bulb in the bathroom?

   _____

7. Could they put their garbage in the hall? _____

2 *Ann is telling Amy and Rick about her childhood. Look at the pictures. Then complete the conversation with* **would** *or* **wouldn't**. *Remember that* **wouldn't** *is the contraction for* **would not**.

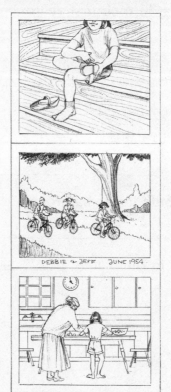

ANN: As soon as the school year ended, I _____ go to my grandparents'
1
house in Chanute. I remember that when I got there, I _____
2
take off my shoes and I _____ go without shoes almost all
3
summer. My grandfather was a country doctor, and every morning I
_____ get up at 5:00 and go with him to visit his patients. Then
4
I _____ come home for breakfast and then go out to play with
5
my friends. We _____ play games or ride our bikes, and sometimes
6
we _____ go fishing. Usually I _____ get home until
7 8
dinner time—sometimes later!

RICK: _____ you go out with your grandpa every day?
9

ANN: Almost. I _____ go with him on Saturdays or Sundays. On
10
Saturday I _____ always help Grandma cook, and on Sunday
11
we _____ all go to church.
12

3 Look at the pictures. Then write the correct sentence in each bubble.

- Would you help me with my homework?
- Could you take these to the cleaners for me?
- Would you please stop talking?
- Could you open this for me?

1.

2.

3.

4.

GRAMMAR BOX

could and *would*

Could and *would* are modals and do not change in form.

1. Use *could*
   a. as the simple past tense of *can*, showing ability: I could swim 5 miles when I was 18, but now I can't swim more than 100 yards.
   b. for polite requests: Could you open the door for me?
   c. for permission: Could I have a drink of water?

2. Use *would*
   a. to show repeated actions in the past, meaning "used to": I would stay out late every Saturday night when I was in high school.
   b. for polite requests: Would you pass the sugar, please?
   c. as the simple past of *will:* He said he'd call.
   d. in the negative, to show that someone refuses to do something: I asked him to help me, but he wouldn't.

4 *Look at the pictures and write sentences about what Amy and Rick could or couldn't do when they were five. You might want to use these words:* swim, ride a bicycle, play baseball, play the piano, sing, read, write, play video games.

1. When Amy was five ___she could read_____, but
   ___she couldn't write._____

2. _____, but
   _____

3. _____, but
   _____

4. When Rick was five, _____, but
   _____

5. _____, but
   _____

6. _____, but
   _____

Now you're ready for the computer. When you finish at the computer, go to the next page.

5 *Look at the pictures and complete the sentences with* **couldn't** *or* **wouldn't**.

1. I asked Pete to give me a ride, but

he _____.

2. I asked Pete to give me a ride, but

he _____.

3. Dick wanted to watch TV, but he

_____.

4. I asked Dick to watch TV with me,

but he _____.

5. Frank asked Nell to help him, but

she _____.

6. Frank asked Nell to help him, but

she _____.

6 Complete these sentences about yourself.

1. When I was four, I could already _____.

2. By the time I was twelve, I could _____.

3. I couldn't _____ before I was _____.

4. I couldn't _____ until I was _____.

5. When I was in elementary school, I would _____
_____.

6. I wouldn't _____ until I was _____.

7 Write questions you would like to ask a friend about his or her childhood or youth. For example:

Could you read before you went to school?
Could you type by the time you went to college?

1. _____

2. _____

3. _____

4. _____

5. _____

8 Write a paragraph about things you did (you would do) when you were younger.

_____

_____

_____

_____

_____

1 *Victoria Finley is very rich. She always gives her family and friends wonderful Christmas presents. Look at the pictures. Then try to guess what she's going to give each person this year and complete the sentences. There are many possible answers.*

Victoria

Sandra,
Victoria's daughter

Mark,
Victoria's son

Jeffrey,
Victoria's son

Claire and Ralph,
Victoria's parents

George,
Victoria's friend

1. I think she's going to give the ____stereo____ to ____Jeffrey____.

2. She's probably going to buy the _____ for_____.

3. I think she's going to send the _____ to _____.

4. She's probably going to give the _____ to_____.

5. I think she's going to buy the _____ for_____.

6. I hope she gives the _____ to me.

7. I hope she sends the _____ for me and my family / husband / wife.

Now write the sentences in another way. For example:

I think she's going to give ___ *Jeffrey* ___ the ___ *stereo* ___ .

1. _____

2. _____

3. _____

4. _____

5. _____

2 *Victoria finally made her decision. Complete the sentences with* **me, us, him, her,** *or* **them.**

1. Victoria knew that Sandra lived in a very cold place, so she gave _____ the fur coat.

2. She knew that Mark liked to go camping in the hills around his house, so she bought _____ the jeep.

3. She knew that her parents had a lot of free time and they liked to travel, so she gave _____ the trip to China.

4. She knew that George liked beautiful jewelry, so she bought _____ the gold watch.

5. She knew that I liked _____ , so she gave _____ the _____ .

6. She knew that my family and I liked _____ , so she sent _____ the _____ .

3 Complete the conversations with it, them, some, *or* one.

1. **A:** Have you sent your parents your graduation picture?

   B: Of course. I sent _____ to them last week.

2. **A:** Jane, give Billy some popcorn.

   B: But, Mom, I've already given him _____ .

3. **A:** Where did Beth get those beautiful earrings?

   B: Her mother made _____ for her.

4. **A:** I really have more pens than I need.

   B: Could you lend me _____ , please?

5. **A:** Why does Petey have those potato chips?

   B: Mom bought _____ for him.

Direct and Indirect Objects

1. There are three patterns for word order with direct and indirect objects.

A	indirect object	direct object
She sent	her father	some roses.
She bought	him	some roses.

B	direct object		indirect object
She sent	some roses	to	her father.

C	direct object		indirect object
She bought	some roses	for	him.

2. Use either placement **A** or **B** with the verbs *bring, give, lend, sell, send, take,* and *tell.*

3. Use either placement **A** or **C** with the verbs *buy, find, get,* and *make.*

4. Never use placement **A** if both pronouns are definite. (Definite pronouns are *me, you, him, her, it, them, us.*)

   Did he give it to you?

5. You can use placement **A**, however, if either the direct or indirect object is an indefinite pronoun (*one, some*) or a demonstrative pronoun (*this, that, these, those*).

   She gave me some.
   Can you give him these?

4 *Read the sentences. Then look at the ads and write the correct sentence in each ad.*

- Please give this child a college education.
- When was the last time you bought him something special?
- Have you sent her flowers lately?
- Make them a surprise tonight.
- Buy your children U.S. savings bonds.
- Sell us your old car.

1. Have you sent her flowers lately?

FLORISTS INTERNATIONAL

2. 908 Four-Wheel Drive
Lawrence
Tel. 555-9005

JOE'S USED CARS

3. MARYDALE Dark Chocolate Cake Mix

4. Give to your favorite scholarship fund.

5. U.S. SAVINGS BOND $1000.00

6. SPELLMAN WATCHES

Now write the ads in a different way.

1. _____ Please give a college education to this child. _____

2. _____

3. _____

4. _____

5. _____

6. _____

5 *Bob is trying to decide what to get Ann for her birthday. He's talking to a friend. Complete the conversation, putting the words in parentheses in the correct order. Use to or for if necessary.*

ARI: Why don't you give her flowers?

BOB: No. I bought _____ last week.
                              (1. her / some)

ARI: Well, she wanted that silver ring she saw at the jeweler's on Main Street.

BOB: I know. I bought _____ last month, for our anniversary.
                                (2. her / it)

ARI: Well, she's been talking about getting a cat. Why don't you get

_____ now?
        (3. her / one)

BOB: That's a good idea! I might even get her two. I'll get

_____ tomorrow night. Thanks!
        (4. her / them)

Now you're ready for the computer. When you finish at the computer, go to the next page.

103

6 *Complete the conversations with a direct and an indirect object pronoun. Use* **to** *or* **for** *when necessary.*

1. **SUE:** What a beautiful ring!

   ANN: Thank you. Bob gave _____.

2. **PAM:** My husband never gives me flowers.

   ANN: That's too bad. Bob gives me flowers all the time. He gave _____

   just last week.

3. **ANN:** Your father saw a watch he really loves.

   RICK: I know. I think I'll buy _____ for his birthday.

4. **BOB:** Are those running shoes for Rick?

   ANN: Yes. I got _____ for his birthday.

5. **AMY:** Where did Dad get that beautiful tie pin?

   RICK: I made _____.

   AMY: Really?

   RICK: Yes. In a class at school.

6. **AMY:** (*on the phone*) Grandpa, I think I left my calculator at your house last week.

   BILL: You sure did. I'll send _____ tomorrow morning.

7 *Think of a day when you give presents. Then answer these questions.*

1. What would you like to give your parents?

   _____

2. What would you like to get for your sister or brother?

   _____

3. What would you like to buy your best friend?

   _____

4. What would you like to send to another friend?

   _____

5. What would you like to get your husband / wife / girlfriend / boyfriend?

   _____

1 *Look at the pictures. Then complete the sentences with the phrases in the box.*

learned how to make tools	started painting and drawing pictures
started wearing clothes	begun to grow food
started living in big cities	started hunting in groups
discovered how to make fire	learned how to cook food
developed a written language	started building houses

1. By the end of the Ice Age in Europe, human beings had already __learned__ __how to make tools.__

2. They had _____

3. They had _____

4. They had _____

5. They had _____

6. They had _____

7. They had _____

8. By the end of the Ice Age in Europe, human beings hadn't _____

_____ yet.

9. They hadn't _____ yet.

10. They hadn't _____ yet.

2 *Choose one of the sentences in the box to describe each picture.*

1. _____

2. _____

> When Linda got home, Phil was cleaning house.
> When Martha got home, Jack had already cleaned the house.

3. _____

4. _____

> We had just finished dinner when the O'Rourkes arrived.
> We were still eating dinner when the Andersons arrived.

5. _____

_____

6. _____

_____

> Dick had already gotten out of the car when the police arrived.
> When the police arrived, Jim was getting out of the car.

7. _____

_____

8. _____

_____

> It was raining when we left the house.
> It had already stopped raining when we left the house.

9. _____

_____

10. _____

_____

> The pilot had already started the propeller when we got into the helicopter.
> After we got into the helicopter, the pilot started the propeller.

GRAMMAR BOX

Past Perfect

1. Use *had* + past participle to form the past perfect tense.

2. The past perfect shows a past action that was completed before another past action.

   Amy had already done her homework when her parents got home.

3. Notice how questions are formed:

   Victor **had** finished lunch by the time we arrived.

   Had Victor   finished lunch by the time you arrived?

   Yes,   he   **had.**

4. If the first action was not completed when the second action occurred, use the past progressive.

   Victor was eating lunch when we arrived.

---

3 *Ann left a note for Rick and Amy, telling them what they should do around the house. As they did each job, they crossed it off the list. Read the list. Then write sentences about what they had done and hadn't done by the time their mother got home.*

~~Clean the bathrooms~~
~~Water the plants~~
Take out the garbage
Get the clothes at the cleaners
~~Cut the grass~~
~~Sweep the front porch~~
Start dinner
~~Vacuum the family room~~
Defrost the refrigerator
Wash the living-room windows
Dust
~~Feed the dogs~~

1.   When Ann got home, Rick and Amy had already cleaned the bathroom, but they hadn't gotten the clothes at the cleaners yet.

2.

3.

4.

5.

6.

Now you're ready for the computer. When you finish at the computer, go to the next exercise.

4 *Look at the information about Mozart, the Austrian composer. Then use the past perfect of the verbs in parentheses to complete the paragraph.*

> **Wolfgang Amadeus Mozart (1756–1791)**
> **1759** Could play chords on the piano
> **1760** Could memorize and play short pieces of music
> **1762** Wrote his first compositions
> **1762** Played before the royal family of Austria
> **1763** Performed for Louis XV of France
> **1768** Composed his first opera and two symphonies
> **1768** Became concertmaster for the archbishop of
>   Salzburg and began writing church music

By the time Mozart was three, he _____ to play chords on the piano;
            (1. learn)

by the time he was four, he _____ to play short pieces of music.
            (2. learn)

When he was eight, he already _____ his first compositions and
            (3. write)

_____ the piano before the royal families of Austria and France. By the
      (4. play)

time he was 13, he _____ an opera and two symphonies, and he
            (5. write)

_____ the concertmaster for the archbishop of Salzburg.
      (6. become)

5 *Complete this article, using either the past progressive or the past perfect of the verbs in parentheses.*

Boy Drowns and Comes Back to Life!

Marty Johnson _____ near Grant Lake last Thursday evening
(1. play)

when he decided to walk out on the ice that was covering the lake. He

_____ just _____ onto the ice when it broke and he
(2. step)

fell into the ice-cold water. He sank to the bottom of the lake. A friend saw the

accident and called the police. When they arrived, Marty _____
(3. be)

under water for 20 minutes. By the time they got him out, he _____
(4. be)

under water for 40 minutes. They thought he was dead, but they took him to a

hospital. Six hours later Marty _____ up in bed and _____
(5. sit)   (6. talk)

to his parents!

The doctors explained what _____ to Marty. When he fell into
(7. happen)

the icy water, his body became cold very quickly, and his bodily functions

_____ down. By the time the police found him, he _____
(8. slow)   (9. stop)

breathing, but his heart had never _____ beating. The doctors
(10. stop)

heated his body up very slowly and he lived.